Terry John Woods'

Farmhouse Modern

Terry John Woods'

Farmhouse Modern

Written with Dale West

Photographs by Kindra Clineff

Stewart, Tabori & Chang, New York

Published in 2013 by Stewart, Tabori & Chang
An imprint of ABRAMS

Library of Congress Control Number: 2013935992

ISBN: 978-1-61769-031-0

Editor: Dervla Kelly
Designer: Tim Preston
Production Manager: Tina Cameron

The text of this book was composed in Gill Sans

Printed and bound in China
10 9 8 7 6 5 4 3 2 1

Stewart, Tabori & Chang books are available at special
discounts when purchased in quantity for premiums
and promotions as well as fundraising or educational use.
Special editions can also be created to specification.
For details, contact specialsales@abramsbooks.com
or the address below.

THE ART OF BOOKS SINCE 1949
115 West 18th Street
New York, NY 10011
www.abramsbooks.com

Contents

Introduction 6

Decorative Simplicity 8

Edgy Antiquities 52

Uniquely Common 92

Group of One 116

Tarnished Perfection 154

Tinsel and Tin 202

Introduction

Farmhouse Modern highlights my favorite elements of design and style in a new light. Traditional Farmhouse style was such an influence in my early years as a designer and remains close to my heart; but I also now find myself drawn to the lines and elements of modern and industrial design pieces. My first inclination was that common ground of these two distinct styles was unlikely to be found. But I quickly learned that by playing these contrasting elements against each other, I could achieve a new and interesting focus. The painted pine furniture that fits into the farmhouse like a piece in a puzzle is now a piece of interesting art when seen as a focal point among complementary contemporary accents. *Farmhouse Modern* honors tradition while offering some ideas for transforming a traditional look into something a bit more current and fresh. It's my hope that *Farmhouse Modern* will lead you to an opportunity to see and appreciate your home and furnishings as if for the first time.

Decorative

Simplicity

Less really is more. Common items are reinvented through creative placement in your home while unadorned spaces serve as frames in which to display your favorite pieces as visual art.

A modestly sized traditional wing chair takes on a contemporary look when slip-covered in white canvas. Placement of the chair directly under the large window is a modern style that gives an illusion of space created by the scale of both objects.

I am surprised when I look back through photographs from not so many years ago to see how my style preferences have changed and evolved over the years. There was a time when I felt somewhat uncomfortable with empty spaces in my decorating and design work. It was as though these sparse spaces were unfinished and begging to display just the right piece. My approach to design then was like piecing together an intricate puzzle of complementary colors and forms. There weren't many surprises, it was easy on the eye, and, like a puzzle, you knew what the overall picture was going to be.

More recently, I have developed an appreciation for the power of empty spaces. The white space left on the artist's canvas and the anticipatory silence intentionally written into a symphonic masterpiece are integral parts of a creative work. The same consideration should be given the space surrounding the elements in your design scheme. Frame your focal pieces in space and appreciate them for the form and color that may have been overshadowed or lost in a less ordered arrangement.

When I began to remove the chaos of clutter, I began to appreciate the intrinsic beauty in the most common pieces: the artistry of handcrafted pine, the graceful lines and patina of an ironstone pitcher, and the simple cupboard with a vibrant wash of paint chipped and worn by time.

At about this same time I began to develop an interest in and appreciation for contemporary design. The simple, clean lines and industrial feel of that style certainly stand in dramatic contrast to the primitive farmhouse pieces that have filled my home and my heart for years. I began to play with these two unique styles: sharp lines juxtaposed with intricate hand-turned wood; the naturally muted hues of a milk-paint wash versus vibrant, intense synthetic color; and natural fabrics working alongside plastic, leather, and steel.

The overall impact of working these styles together effectively highlights unique qualities of each. I started seeing interior design as less about furniture placement or color choice and more about focus, contrast, and space.

During a recent drive along the coast of Maine, I pulled over to admire a field filled with a wide variety of wildflowers of all colors, textures, and sizes. The overall effect was that of a single stunning, brightly colored mass. There was no differentiating between varieties and individual plants; this meadow appeared to be one large bloom. When I returned home, I was drawn to the yellow daylilies by the back door; I picked one and placed it in a simple clear vase. It struck me that the difference between the meadow of color and the single bloom I brought into the house beautifully illustrates the changes in my approach to and appreciation for design. There are so many interesting elements that go unappreciated and overlooked when our senses are overwhelmed. Start with a focus on the single work of art, the single most masterful turn in a piece of handmade furniture, and the perfect bloom in the floral arrangement and build your design outward from there. You will be amazed, as I have been, that your sensibilities will change with time and you will see more in less.

I will always have a place in my heart for primitive furniture. I love the worn, dry painted surfaces and rich colors and of course that "one of a kind" peace of mind that it is just mine! Here, a collection of yellow ware bowls appreciated for their form, color, and imperfections is lined up side by side and arranged like modern sculptures on a prized red-painted country cupboard.

My motto is that "any space is fair game for styling," especially when trying to lend an unexpected modern edge to an area. Here a collection of old toy boats painted an eye-catching bright turquoise is placed single file across an idle love seat in this bedroom sitting area. The repeating forms of the vintage mini sculptures along with the textured wood surfaces contrast with the heavy white canvas fabric, visually creating pops of color.

In my Vermont studio, my design approach has never changed: less is more and simple is better. This sofa, previously covered in a bold patterned fabric, now sports a white canvas slipcover that simplifies its curved lines. The small, round pedestal table originally finished in dark oak has a lighter look with a fresh coat of light gray paint, while the chipped green and white garden urn creates a focal point in the room by adding texture, scale, and just enough color.

Our large pantry cupboard in our Vermont house was found at a nunnery on the seacoast of Massachusetts. The "ark" of the piece was painted a pumpkin orange when purchased and was quickly transformed with a coat of light gray paint. The storage piece fades into the background, showcasing on its top my collection of ironstone bowls that long ago lost their pitchers. Make sure to keep your collections organized and simple to achieve a contemporary attitude.

A rustic tin-top garden table separates the couch and chair in our family room. A plant in an urn placed as a focal point when you enter the room rests centered in the window, adding a sense of order to the corner. The room's pale color is enhanced by one of my large, colorful modern abstract paintings that dominates the wall over the small sofa. The large painting combined with the oversize couch pillows creates a scale that borders on modern whimsy.

A pale gray Swedish-style sofa corrals a group of different-size, plump down pillows covered in fabrics ranging from antique linen to worn cotton. Revisit and repurpose your old linens as options for pillows, window treatments, or slipcovers.

Pillows stacked flat on a sofa or chair will create an abstract look, especially when used to update traditional pieces. Here, a wonderful down sofa with a graphic covering gets a visual update with this simple pillow placement.

Three large lantern globes of antique curved, tinted glass create a modern-looking visual when lined up in a row on the table. Each holds a simple sphere made from handblown glass or leather, adding form and color to the unadorned white space.

An old "cellar hole find" bottle is used as a simple but creative vase. By keeping the flower placement low and the water level to a minimum, the bottle shines with a new artistic value while adding a visual that is unexpected and sleek.

Garden decoratives are readily available, and most have luscious patinas covering their unique shapes. This collection, organized by soothing pale colors and richly weathered textures, is arranged like fine art. The collection includes sculptural wooden finials, weathered sculptured bowls filled with fruit, and an overscale cement plaque, all of which add to the neutral modern look.

An unexpected arrangement of antiques harmonizes well due to their green theme. The textural primitive cupboard serves as a shelf for a summery bovine painting, while an early octagonal terrarium holding a single shell is placed offset, giving a contemporary feel to the vignette.

The huge window in our upstairs hall landing is grounded by a clean-lined, slipcovered sofa. The oversize rough linen pillows add scale, texture, and comfort to the small space. A "flea market find" pharmacy lamp that once sported a brassy gold finish was spray-painted silver and distressed with steel wool to give it a less assuming presence.

A common steel-mesh trash container is repurposed as contemporary art in the farmhouse's side hall. Combined with the bold black-and-white floor, a moss sphere, and an underscale traditional painting, an unassuming space takes on a repurposed current attitude.

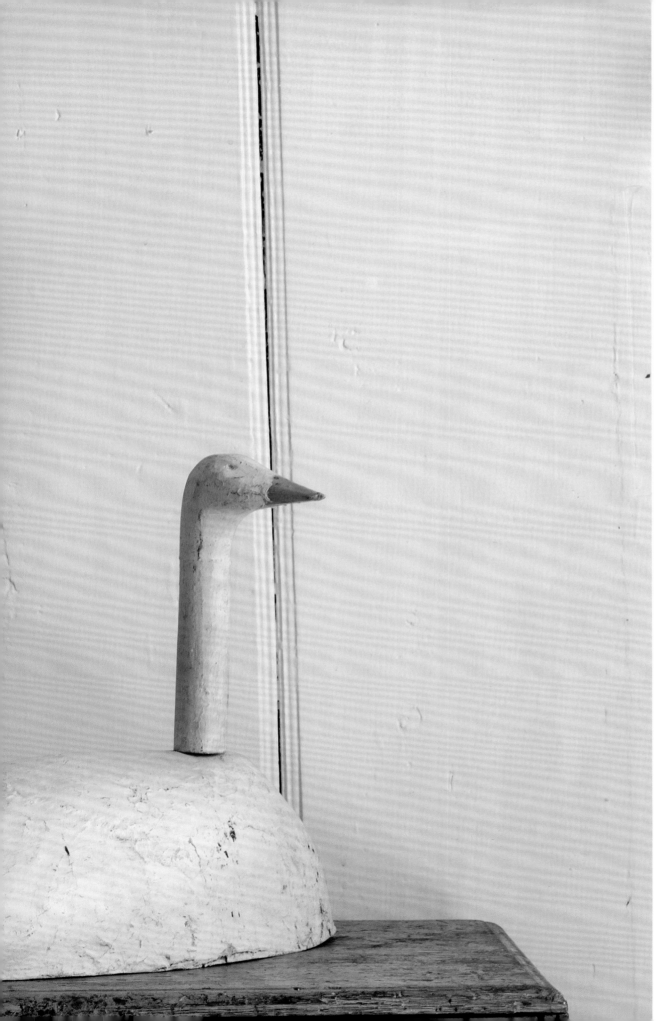

Collections are defined as a group of two or more. Keeping a display of a collection to a minimum showcases the items so they can be appreciated singularly. Here, a collection of geese, one antique and one newly carved, are combined with a rustic newel post that adds height and texture to the whimsical vignette.

A once-fussy Victorian sofa has been re-created into a softer, updated, modern-edged piece. The dark walnut trim has been painted a pale gray and the heavy tapestry upholstery replaced with vintage white linen. The sofa's unique lines can be appreciated even more due to the uncluttered space around it.

I adore texture and strive to bring it forward in a room's design. Here, a round pewter charger with a dull silver finish is combined with a gleaming white ironstone bowl and placed strategically in front of a three-dimensional distressed paneled wall. The round shapes and graphic squares contribute to the abstract approach.

Gleaming light shines through a bedroom sitting area, placing focus on a pair of vintage wicker chairs covered with antique French linen. A quirky Adirondack table holds two "auction find" tarnished trophies that add height and curved forms to the graphic space.

At our farmhouse, fresh yellow flowers and lemons are placed on the old enamel sink drainboard in the kitchen. In the distance, at right, the blue dining room cupboard harmonizes with the daisies' yellow hues, creating a soothing, fresh look in the otherwise neutral-colored space

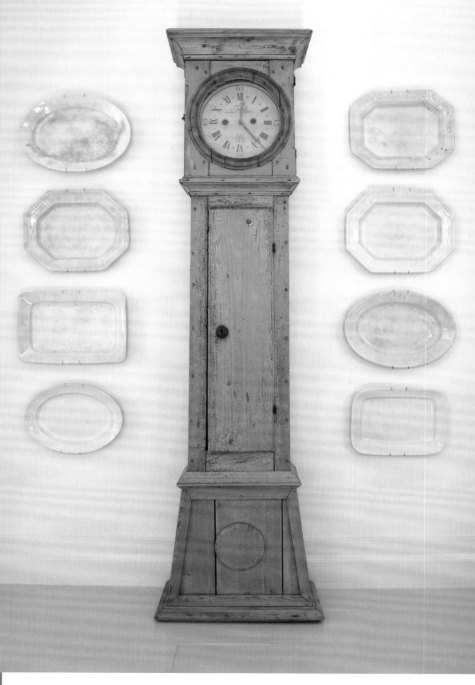

An early 19th century swedish clock boasting a pale, distressed, pine patina adds visual height to our Vermont dining room. Ironstone platters of varying shapes and sizes in mottled white colors are hung one above the other, creating an artistic detail which frames the tall clock on either side.

The living room of our Vermont house is flanked by huge rippled-glass windows in the white walls, creating a sense of light and airiness. Canvas-covered seating filled with linen-covered down pillows, along with the white textural shapes of finials, all seem to fade into the white space. Even white birch logs, stacked vertically on their ends, add to the modern farmhouse feel.

In our guest bedroom, a pale gray four-poster bed layered with simple textured linens and smooth cotton pillows stacked high creates a welcoming place of rest.

Color-matched pillows work best when the colors are light, the fabric has texture, and patterns are at a minimum. Keeping color palettes similar creates an illusion of space.

A mid-century iron and vinyl chair paired with a turquoise tiled floor adds color and form to this traditional side porch. The graphic lines of the slatted window grate at left along with the horizontal wood siding and the grout lines in the floor present bold visual patterns that add to the room's modern graphic design.

A striped canvas pillow in neutral colors adds dimension to this white-based living room. The straight lines in the pillow's fabric combined with the flowing shapes of the ironstone pitchers in the background add a geometric feel.

Outdoor garden areas need focal points too. Here, a large rust-covered urn stands alone in the garden as sculpture, with its newly planted sphere giving a modern twist to the formal piece, which can be seen from all parts of the outdoor space.

Large, weathered cement globes trail along in an abstract
pattern on the garden's edge, adding whimsy to the space.

A mid-twentieth-century iron dining chair painted in classic black takes on a new purpose as a makeshift plant stand in our Vermont courtyard. The French enamel bucket creates a simple planter for the red geraniums while adding shape and texture to the setting.

Seasonal spring paperwhites are planted in simple makeshift burlap pots. Grouped together, their subtle pops of color and earthly scents add brightness to the dimly lit space.

A pale gray repurposed iron form adds height to the garden while lessening the visual space available with its airy construction. Its contemporary lines and abstract appearance contrast with the antique wooden finial, adding a modern art sculpture approach to the garden.

Farmhouse

A wire-mesh chair and a brightly colored collection of vintage pottery speak volumes about the modern-edge design of this space, while the rustic painted wood floor adds a backdrop of minimal texture.

A clean-lined entry hall is visually painted by the bold abstract fabric covering the seating space. The ornate mirror frame complements the fabric while reflecting the small space, giving it a larger, modern look.

I am attracted to industrial pieces because of their strong construction, metal finishes, and contemporary style and use them when possible in my design space. Here, a richly painted blue factory chair is unexpectedly added to an eighteenth-century keeping room. The sleek lines of the chair complement the lines of the grid-patterned wood wall, while a collection of worn cotton American flags softens the space by adding layers of fabric and color.

A vintage curved French sofa gets a contemporary look by adding a loosely fitted canvas slipcover and oversize down pillows. Combined with an abstract painting of soft grays with white and an artist-made copper floor lamp, the room now has an updated style while most of the pieces in the space have been repurposed.

A brightly colored modern painting commands the area behind a simple white lamp. The large scale of the painting combines with the undersized shade to blend and create a modern look.

The sleek-lined sofa covered in a pale twill fabric hosts just a single pillow alongside the brick chimney, which, combined with the rustic wood-planked walls, gives this farmhouse living space a modern "city loft" look.

Small-scale prints hang high in a row, creating the look of a single piece of linear art. A formal English table is softened with an antique galvanized bucket placed slightly off-center and appreciated for its modern industrial sculptural shape.

Edgy Antiquities

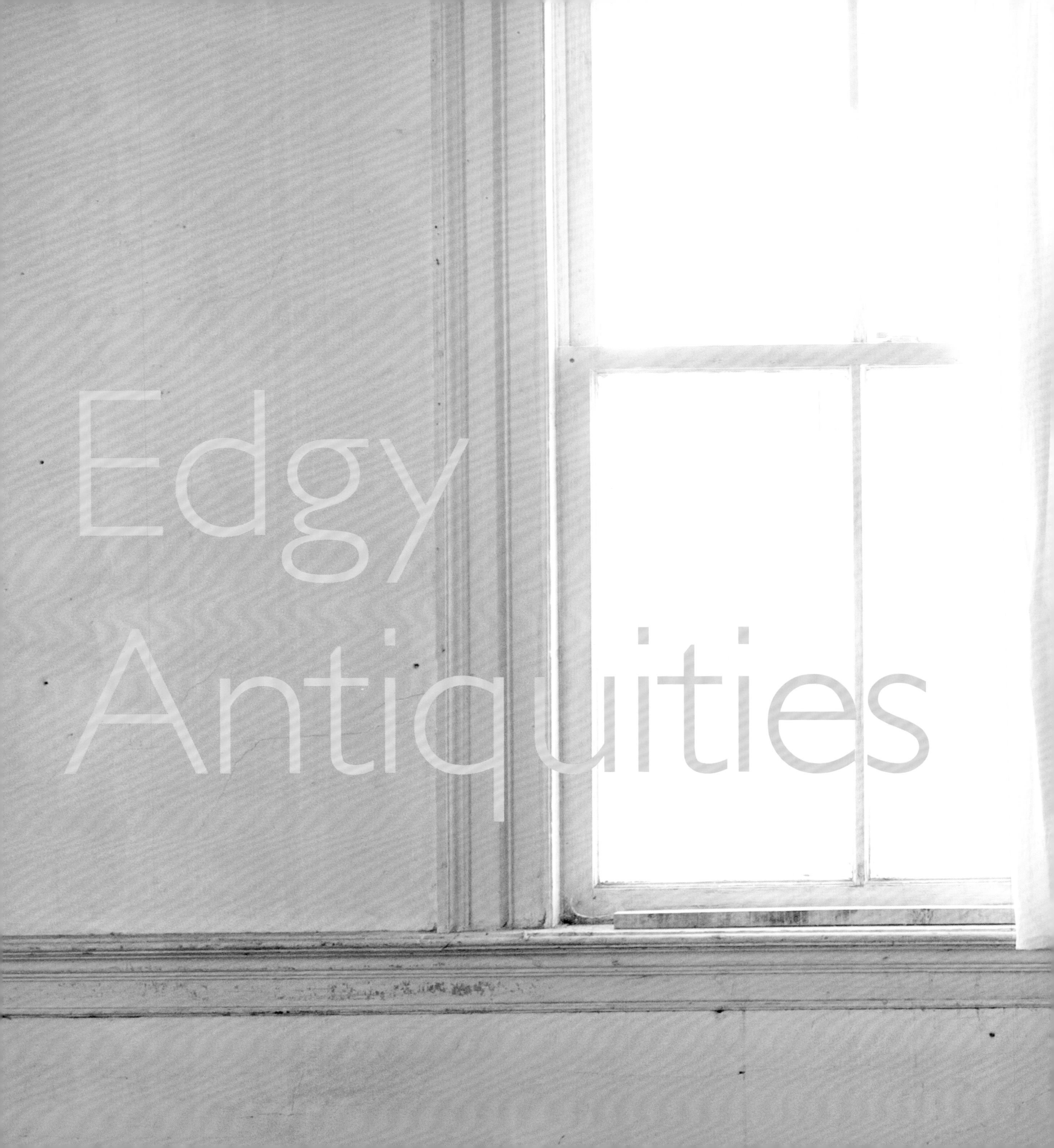

The elements of modern design may be best appreciated when combined with more traditional components. Sleek-lined furnishings paired with a farmhouse antique will create a visual contrast, bringing new focus to the unique qualities each piece has to offer.

Found at a local factory sale, this industrial metal cupboard painted bright blue hosts many uses on the farmhouse porch. The clunky, heavy piece is used as a server for quiet dinners by night and corralling gardening supplies by day. Metal pieces like this work well outside because they stand up to inclement weather and are useful for extra outdoor storage.

A design purist who carefully seeks out pieces for a particular style or period may very well shudder upon finding a 1950s-era modern chair purposely paired with an 1800s primitive pie safe or a modern abstract oil painting perched atop the chipped-paint pine armoire. I'll have to admit that my own sensibilities were put to the test when I began to mix styles that stand in such contrast with one another. I now look for opportunities to blend the new with the old where I can create a sense of conflict with my choices of color, form, and style.

For example, the hard steel frame of a modern chair can serve as a frame and canvas for a painted pine piece. The unique design elements of each piece complement and highlight the form and color of the other. The effect of these pairings is an artistic edginess that I enjoy. Using a piece of furniture that is traditional or customary in another setting is both unexpected and bold when combined in this contrasting manner. A functional sculpture now exists where a table and lamp may have stood before, no less useful but perhaps more visually interesting and artistically stimulating.

Paint is my friend. A light wash of paint can make an older piece suddenly seem more current and be more relevant in my design plan. I have experimented with silver paint to give an edgy look to a piece that has become tired and uninspiring. I find that these techniques are most effective in moderation. An unexpected splash of color or a more contemporary finish on a vintage piece opens the door for creative expression where you would least expect it. In a recent kitchen upgrade, I found the perfect-size piece to use as an island. The old map chest had several shallow drawers that had once been used to hold maps. This piece now provides plenty of kitchen storage and, once topped with a new piece of glossy white Carrara marble, it took on a timeless quality. Look for opportunities to create your own style with simple updates.

I plan carefully to maintain a frame of space around groupings, pairings, and individual elements of design. This space, much like that created around pieces in an art gallery, creates an area of focus and confers a sense of order to your design. Start with a couple of your favorite pieces that speak to you but may argue with each other, then mediate and experiment to see if you can create something unique with the qualities they possess.

The small den in our Vermont house is my favorite room. We had planned originally to make it our kitchen, but the space was inadequate. Two huge windows hug the old boarded-up fireplace in the room, letting gleaming north light in all day long. Slipcovered French chairs and creamy white trim add to the bright space. An old palladium window found in Maine adds dimension and height to the space, while the sisal rug on the floor marries the two with the same wood tones as the window frame.

Formal furnishings, including a polished drop side table and a low-backed leather sofa, are given a contemporary edge by adding bright turquoise in the form of a large-scale lamp shade, down pillows, and a pair of whimsical artistic chickens.

Symmetry is very important for creating visual balance in a design space. In our living room, our formal camelback sofa is centered between two tall pillars that add boundaries and height to the room. Resting upon an early English blanket box is an abstract nude painting that adds bright color and a modern twist to the traditional space.

A collection of early Staffordshire dogs lines the primitive mantel, while a farm scene painted by a local artist hangs just above. The linear painting complements the length of the mantel while the formal porcelain mixed with the contemporary art creates an unlikely marriage that works!

I found this early reproduction Windsor chair at a local flea market. I loved the lines of the chair but wanted it to be received in a more modern way. I have always used silver as a complementary color throughout our Vermont house, so I decided to spray it silver. Instant success! I love the contemporary edge it now has, and its patina gets better the more it is used.

Pieces stacked one upon another creates a modern way of displaying things in a group. Here, a large weathered porch finial has been repurposed into a gallery-type pedestal in the living room of the farmhouse. The animal-themed collection of an early porcelain chicken and an abstract painting of prized goats is a reminder of what's roaming just outside the door.

This mid-century aluminum floor lamp with an adjustable-height base, lightweight construction, and directional lamp head is very useful while also adding a modern flair to the room.

The once-dark oak T-back chairs take on a contemporary edge when painted an unexpected bright yellow and placed in a group around an early tavern table. The unframed "flea market find" painting of flowers in golden hues harmonizes with the chairs, creating even more vibrant and intense color.

A pale yellow pedal car found in Texas made its way to the East Coast and now sits high atop a cupboard in a friend's living room. The pale colors of the room combined with the white cupboard and robin's-egg blue wooden chest create a soothing, upscale, and unexpected modern grouping.

A friend's antique home on the coast is filled with many collections of primitive antiques, modern art, silver, and rare French porcelain. I admire the way she is able to combine all these unlikely things and make them work as a group. In her dining room, a formal Sheridan sideboard creates a shelf for a funky art pottery coral vase. Along the wall is a vibrant painting of a lobster paired with the soft texture of an oversize galvanized bucket, creating a casual but structured edgy design.

Two sleek-lined chairs covered in Belgian linen are placed tightly together under a large graphic painting in a bedroom reading area. The placement of the chairs and the art placed slightly askew gives the room an artistic flair while creating a cozy nook to read in.

Brightly colored oranges dance across the tabletop of an early one-drawer stand while a pair of ornamental trees are symmetrically placed under a primitive painting that towers over the natural vignette.

An unlikely grouping of wall art consisting of early paintings and a "rare find" white stop sign creates a playful way of mixing art with form and texture.

Three old soda fountain stools are now used as sleek modern pedestals. The vintage bottles grouped together create an artful display of shape and color alongside the barnyard sitting area.

A mid-century canary yellow garden chair takes center stage in the farmhouse living room. The piece, appreciated for its bold graphic lines, scalloped edges, and gently curved arms, adds to the visual concept underpinning the room.

Touches of bright color in a room can intensify the space while also adding a contemporary flair. Here, a group of mid-century chairs covered in coral pink vinyl with strong iron fret designs paired with a graphic slatted window are visually softened by the vibrant blue ceiling and round matching blue pillows.

Layering is an effective way to change the appearance of an upholstered piece of furniture. A full-size duvet covered in rough linen is folded neatly and draped over the small love seat. The large, thick duvet paired with the small sofa plays with scale, giving a contemporary look to the traditional piece. Another trick is placing large pillows—the more the better—on small-scale upholstered furniture for a more current look.

An industrial stool in my studio leans into a long painted-pine worktable. The graphic wooden grid that was once a focal point in the garden now works as art on the wall, holding wooden spheres.

This incredible chair was an art project for a friend's daughter. The vintage piece was transformed with handwoven cotton fabric in teal and hand-embroidered designs. Placed in a very traditional setting, the chair cheers up the space with its fun approach and lively design aspects. Never overlook furniture because of style or condition, as it can easily be transformed into comfortable, one-of-a-kind art.

A home office is transformed into a modern space with bold complementary graphics and similar neutral tones.

A brightly colored mid-century sofa and chair with straight modern lines and smooth fabrics dominate the living space of this room. The primitive painting, large in scale, adds contrast in color and graphic form to the space.

A regal Empire chest of drawers has been made less formal with a layer of bright blue paint. Early gardening tools collected for their graphic shapes hang above as art, greeting all who enter the farmhouse.

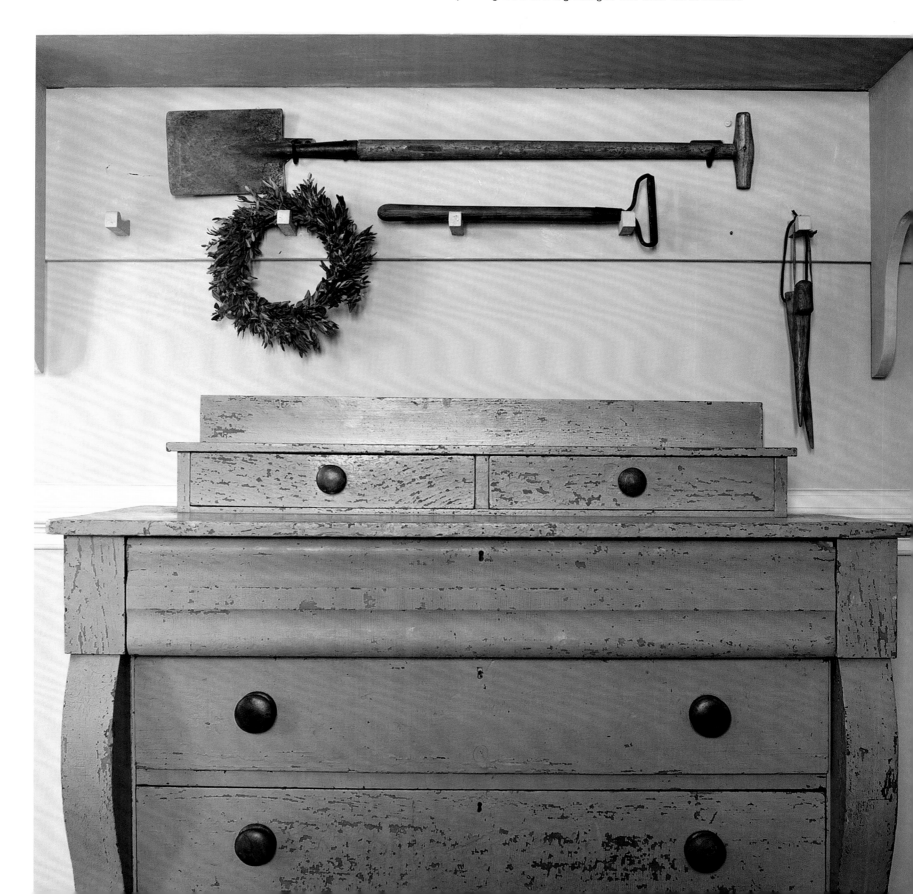

A friend's farmhouse still undergoing the restoration process has wonderful nooks and crannies filled with "one of a kind" textural patinas. Here in the front entry hall, stairs riddled with chipped paint lead upstairs, while a pair of carved dogs watch over a sleek designed chair that adds modern lines to the weathered surroundings.

Our Vermont house required a two-year restoration process. The front entry hall, the biggest project of them all, was saved for last because the railing was long, winding, and held up by many intricate spindles. Once I had stripped it, I was surprised to discover it was made from pine, so I left the light dry finish as a contemporary nod to the old house. The long cupboard was an "antique-store find" that, with its light color and useful storage space, was perfect for the narrow hall. The still life painting, which adds subtle color to the space, suggests a gallery look as it's casually leaned against the wall.

This farmhouse's side porch welcomes all who come to visit. Collections here, arranged by shape, size, and finish, focus on abstract composition, which is achieved with the wire tiered plant stand, the rusted iron garden urn, and the bold graphic letters.

Architectural details and their relationships with interior surroundings are important in a room's design. Here, a simple farmhouse door left unpainted shows textured layers of paint that contrast with the smooth, pale-colored walls. An oil painting, tiny in scale, adds focus to the room's setting.

Two myrtle topiaries placed on a rustic bench create a living sculpture in the front room of the farmhouse. The round forms of the plants soften the strong lines of the paneled walls, while the bench and door complement each other with their similar textures.

A cozy sunporch is the perfect place for this homeowner's collection of antique garden ornaments. The soft palette of colors, which includes gray from the unique garden bench, the putty-colored wooden shutter, the chipped white of the garden urn, and the artistic marble sculptured head, creates an uncluttered modern style when grouped together.

An outdoor area mimics modern art with the combination of some unlikely pieces. A vintage wicker sofa with its original printed fabric creates a backdrop for a group of antique spheres, while an iron plant stand creates a pedestal effect and holds more colorful spheres, adding height to the space. Make sure not to overlook simple shapes. In the right setting and with correct placement, everything has artistic value.

An original mid-century sofa and chair dominate the den with their large scale and vibrant red leather upholstery. The traditional tall clock, single floor lamp, and abstract art bring perfect balance to the room.

A vintage chrome sling chair in black leather adds a contemporary style to the room's neutral corner courtesy of its strong lines and shiny surfaces.

Wood and iron mid-century dining chairs dance across the bright yellow floor of this dining space. Weathered gray walls with strong vertical lines, unadorned sun-filled windows, and large-scale art surround this intimate space, creating a clean-lined mid-century modern feel.

A formal French wall sconce with ornate shades is paired with a contemporary painting of two cows. The unlikely twosome works visually because of their similar size and the unique placement of one above the other.

An antique writing desk freshened with pink and white paint now serves as an open pantry shelf just off the kitchen in the farmhouse. The large painting, which creates a visual focus, complements the desk's color and rectangular shape, while an industrial floor lamp gives much-needed light to this makeshift modern space.

A black antique chimney cupboard stands tall behind a contemporary chaise. The flag is folded narrowly to create an intense vertical design that contrasts with the flowing lines of the chaise. This creates a strong design sense while the complementing reds harmonize the unlikely grouping.

Neutral colors create an illusion of space and are soothing, especially in a bedroom setting. Here, white walls form a backdrop for the multiple down pillows covered in pale-blue-and-white cotton that line the headboard of the tall bed. A modest white bedspread shows off a plump duvet covered in textural sun-bleached rough linen.

A newly purchased big-box-store floor lamp with a modern design is paired with a quirky vintage phone that rests on a small tripod stand in our Vermont farmhouse's guest bedroom.

Common

Refreshing your design might mean repurposing and reincarnating pieces that have been tucked away or become less than interesting. Traditional pieces can take on a second life as art if we just look at these treasures with a new eye. Perhaps this time the focus will be on the object's unique form rather than its intended function.

I like the challenge of repurposing things. I found this inexpensive silver-plated vase at a tag sale. It had a great look with its fluted shape and tarnished imperfections, but I wanted it to have more artistic value. I thought graphics would be interesting with a subtle color painted over them that still let the tarnished silver shine through once they were removed. I applied vinyl adhesive numbers in an abstract design and sprayed the piece with primer gray car paint in a flat finish. The finished art vase is a favorite, and often is filled with seasonal vegetables or simple flower arrangements.

Breaking away from the traditional functions of pieces in your home can be a pretty daunting exercise. We have all tried to shake things up a bit and place a dried flower arrangement in a rusty tin or a weathered box. But hanging chairs on the wall as art or cleaning up the old wire milk bottle crate for towel storage takes a certain amount of creative fortitude and courage.

One really interesting way to start creating with the unexpected is to work with the unknown. There are some wonderful architectural pieces available, maybe a large industrial piece, the intended use of which is lost on most of us. We can study and think and calculate, and really never be able to figure out what on earth this particular thing was actually used for! So rather than intellectualizing and trying to name it, take a look at it for what it is. Many of these pieces have great form; I have seen some great wooden industrial salvage pieces with curved lines, bulky, impressive form, and bold color. Use these treasures as focal pieces; place them as you would a one-of-a-kind bronze sculpture or an exquisite floral arrangement.

Once you have trained yourself to look at objects differently, you will also appreciate color and form in a different way. I have a "sculpture" prominently displayed in our home that always piques others' curiosity and sparks lively debate as to whether it is the headlight off a Model A or a Model T Ford. It is one or the other, and regardless of its origins, it is now appreciated simply as unique art.

"Repurposing" has appeared as a buzzword in design. Putting a name to this design strategy finally makes it chic to bring that cool-looking unidentifiable hunk of rusty iron into your home! A new wave of artists is producing some wildly creative pieces in the name of repurposing. I recently visited a shop that featured only pieces that have been repurposed. Lamps made from old toys, tabletops created from nearly anything flat, and architectural salvage pieces crafted into furniture designs limited only by the maker's imagination. These "new" designs effectively unite the thrill of the flea-market hunt with an introspective visit to a museum of modern art. It's time to open your eyes as if you had never opened them before. Everything really is art.

A rustic blue screened door pie safe holds a collection of serving china in the farmhouse dining room. Whimsically placed early wooden toys are arranged by color and shape, which creates an artistic, modern-edged vignette.

I am always up for the challenge when it comes to mixing different styles in a room. Here, a modern abstract painting hangs offset over a worn, silk-covered Empire sofa, which grounds and gives focus to the room. A vintage modern Parsons table adds bold, straight lines against the curved carved sofa, while a collectible blue dump truck, now appreciated as a work of art, adds a splash of color.

I always look forward to a visit with this special friend of mine, as we are cut from the same cloth, and when we are together, both of us are drenched with artistic abilities. In her dining room is a repurposed sculpture made from found objects that takes center stage. A "flea market find" pond boat set slightly upward is surrounded by white scrolled wooden fretwork creating a stormy-sea effect around it. The repurposed grouping is a perfect addition to her coastal home.

As you enter the farmhouse, a colorful abstract painting hangs low over an intricate button-design chest of drawers. The silver lamp and white tureen are arranged simply on its top, letting the one-of-a-kind graphic chest take center stage in the area.

Different-shaped garden urns serve as containers for wooden spoons and whisks in our Vermont kitchen. The rusty texture and opposing colors add dimension and interest when placed against the polished marble countertops.

Fresh green apples create a whimsical sculpture in the kitchen when placed in a small urn and stacked one on top of another. Try using toothpicks to secure each apple to the next for durability and strength.

Vintage department-store sign holders have new lives as industrial photograph frames. The collection complements the hand-colored early photos with its textured chrome frames of varying heights and widths.

An early tin sugar mold serves as a whimsical picture frame.
Try using multiple molds with family photos in blacks-and-whites,
and arrange them in a group on a table or on the wall.

I have a fondness for wooden carved animals, especially
rocking horses, and use them as much as possible as design
elements in room settings. Sitting on a tabletop in the guest
room is a rare wooden carousel pig from England. Stripped of
its paint to reveal a warm pine patina, the whimsical piece still
sports its iron springlike tail, oversize ears, and dark glass eyes.

A column-base pedestal sink, with its round lines and shiny white finish, now serves as interesting garden decor. Changed seasonally from summer flowers to fall pumpkins and then to winter greens, the sink gives a sense of sculpture to the farmhouse's side lawn.

A one-time porch serving table appreciated for its weathered-gray wood finish and long spindle legs now corrals a collection of bright-green sphere-shaped myrtle topiaries in the garden.

Old weathered clay flowerpots add texture, shape, and soft color to any design scheme. Left empty, they can be appreciated as art especially when grouped together in various sizes. The round cylinders, when stacked high or lined up single file in unexpected areas such as bathrooms or bedrooms or, like here, stacked in a garden chair, add whimsy and visual interest to the space.

Our kitchen in Vermont is newly restored, but still has the atmosphere of being old. A favorite scrubbed pine blanket box complete with mouse holes was once used to store grain for calves on my father's farm. Rescued from the falling-down barn, the weathered piece has now been repurposed as a horizontal pantry under the pot rack in the kitchen.

A long iron industrial worktable with a distressed wooden top is centered in a traditional-style kitchen and serves as a repurposed cook's island. The vinyl-covered mid-century stool, contemporary in design, rolls easily where needed in this finely tuned work space.

An old silver-plated fork handle has been transformed into a whimsical plant stake. Simply stamped with the word "ivy" on its top, the handle, when placed in an old glass inkwell with an ivy cutting, creates a sweet visual on the farmhouse windowsill.

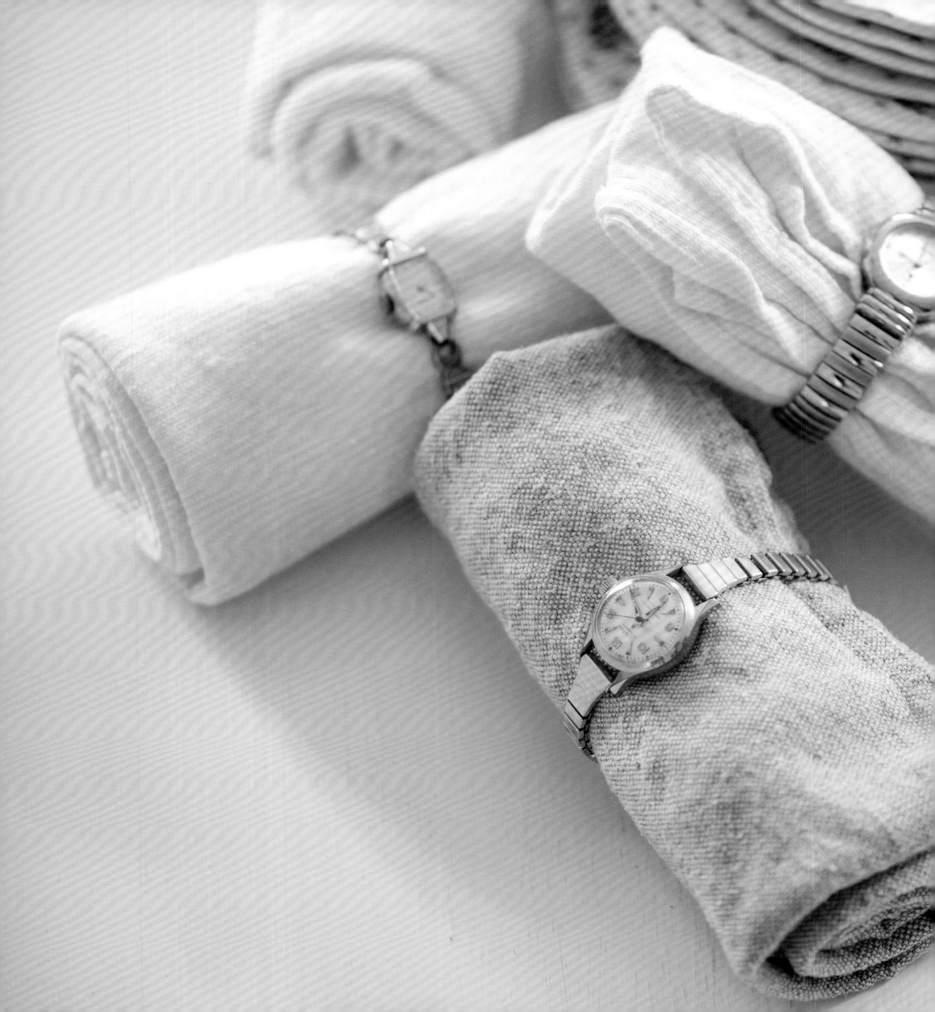

Old petite wristwatches no longer able to keep time have here been cleverly made into interesting dinner-napkin holders. The accordion gold and silver bands allow even the largest rolled napkins to fit. Try this trick: Cut thin paper the same size as the clock face, write the guest's name on it, and affix it to the watch temporarily. This easily directs the seating while the creative concept makes for great dinner conversation.

A vintage galvanized milk carrier complete with its original glass bottles serves as a whimsical flower vase. Here, apple tree branches sporting spring blooms are placed strategically in some bottles while still letting the container be seen and appreciated for the quirky centerpiece it has become.

A bedspring, with its unique shape and rusty iron patina, is repurposed as a sculptural open vase used for holding artist's paintbrushes. The spring's artistic value can be appreciated even more when used as a vase by simply inserting a glass jar inside and adding water and your favorite flower, or as a candleholder by adding a single tea light candle centered in its base, which will cast an abstract reflected shadow when lit.

I found this old automobile headlamp at a flea market and instantly was fond of its large, round shape and clear, shiny multiple-prism lens. I instantly thought "sculpture" and placed it on the bureau in our guest bedroom as a piece of modern art. Once the rusted metal finish was oiled, traces of a black enamel finish that shined through added more to its already dramatic presence.

An apple-green tripod that once stood as a prop in an old legion hall is now repurposed as an airy pedestal in the farmhouse living room. A single white distressed finial sits on its top, creating extra height and artistic focus.

Group of

One

Personal collections have a story that waits to be told. Displaying these treasures is often more challenging than finding them. A well-displayed collection will maximize the effect of the collection as a whole while also allowing individual pieces to shine.

Distressed wooden spools wound with crispy white thread are displayed on a decorative heat radiator. Casually placed, the collection is appreciated for their repeating shapes and textures while adding an artistic charm to the space.

As a child I remember that Sunday afternoons were often set aside for taking a drive. More often than not, this would eventually lead to the carload of us dropping in on a relative. After establishing that we had all grown taller and creeping through secret corners of the attic with cousins who always seemed to know the way, we would settle down to hear the stories that families share over and over and over whenever they are together. It was on one of these visits, and after the grown-ups had started their reminiscing, that I discovered my great aunt's collection of salt and pepper shakers. I first noticed them on a shelf at a six-year-old's eye level. Then I discovered a curio cabinet, more shelves, and entire display cases packed tight with salt and pepper shakers in unimaginable designs. How had I never noticed these treasures before? It was as if a lifeline had been tossed and my rescue from boredom was secure. We all quickly discovered which shakers were completely off-limits and which ones we could use in our own version of Go Fish. As long as they were back where they belonged when we left, they were there for us when we returned on another Sunday afternoon.

To this day, talk about collections takes me back to dusty salt and pepper shakers. Collecting is a passion for many people, but displaying that collection is often a challenge. The bigger the collection, the bigger the challenge. For this reason, I tend to limit the number of items from a collection that I display at one time. Rotating pieces of a collection helps to keep the collection fresh and interesting. For me, the effect that I try to achieve with collections is in the impact as a whole. My collection of ironstone has more in common with a Bach symphony than meets the eye in that it can be appreciated on several levels. Someone familiar with ironstone may pick up on the subtle designs and details of individual pieces, while another observer might respond to the overall presentation. A well-balanced collection has both interesting details and an overall impact. Consider color, texture, and form like you would those of a floral arrangement; you'll know when you have it right.

Industrial pressure gauges with their graphic numbers and metal finishes of brass and stainless steel are simply arranged in a steel divided drawer placed on the wall.

A highly prized collection of French porcelain creates a colorful backdrop in this modern farmhouse kitchen. The collection of three-dimensional art is arranged by height and contrasting shapes, which keeps order in the collection while creating drama.

The collection in this bookcase is based on color alone. Rich red-toned books admired for their decorative hard covers are mixed with other collectibles of the same hues, creating a soothing, unexpected display.

This farmhouse's owner collects delicate antique wooden birdcages in all shapes and sizes. In his guest bedroom, which still has the original wallpaper and paint, are three similar-size cages displayed vertically. This edgy upward arrangement adds visual height to the wall space while highlighting the collection.

I collect vintage flashlights and am constantly searching them out at flea markets and antique shops. I am attracted by their sleek lines, glossy finishes, and many different styles. These tiny sculptures placed in unexpected areas—usually two or three together stacked in a pyramid or simply lined up in a row standing on end—add whimsy to any design space.

A single pocket watch with a pure white face and bold black numerals is displayed in an old, weathered English muffin tin. The silver tones blend together, creating an eye-pleasing collection based on metal finishes.

One of my soft-colored abstract paintings rests low over a primitive cupboard in our Vermont den. A group of white wooden spheres collected for their shape and aged appearance seems to skip across the cupboard's top, adding a layer of texture to the modern-art theme.

Silver-accented lapel brushes from the Victorian Age are now appreciated for their unique shapes, soft textural bristles, and graphic striped colors. Try grouping them in a row on a wall as three-dimensional modern art.

A modest collection of vintage tin geographical globes are grouped in a line on a distressed tabletop. The round spheres of varying sizes and colors imbued with abstract appeal create a modern design in the farmhouse den.

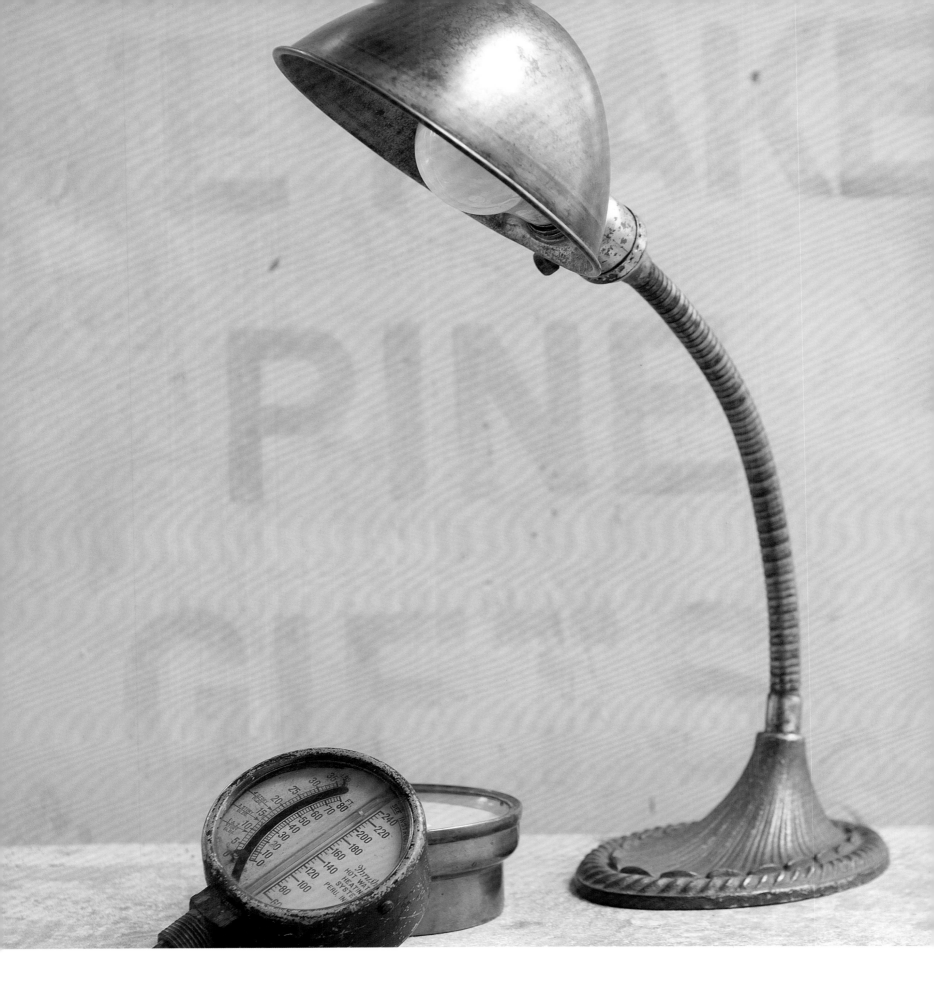

A polished-steel flexible-arm lamp shines over a small group of industrial pressure gauges. The combination of the hard metals and shiny finishes is softened by the faded, boldly lettered sign in the background.

Keys collected for their unique shapes are placed on a silver etched piece of glass that covers a farmhouse bureau top. The combination of similar curves in the keys and in the design in the glass pulls the collection together as a whole.

These rusty green flower frogs were collected for their soft green color, interesting shapes, and one-of-a-kind appeal. The numbered brass and iron sculptures once labeled tables for various social gatherings at a local country club.

A group of favorite vintage tin whistles are displayed simply on a small, white ironstone platter. The richly colored red toile fabric creates a formal backdrop for this unpretentious collection.

One of my larger handmade teddy bears sits alone as a centerpiece on a bright white plank-top farm table. The uncluttered, shiny white table surface makes the bruin a perfect object for attention and appreciation.

Many of my design schemes are based on texture alone. Here, one of my handmade mohair bears is on an old, weathered Adirondack twig table painted a deep blue. Another bear in an opposing color is in an old ironstone footed bowl, adding height to the arrangement while the shiny reflective bowl adds yet another layer of texture.

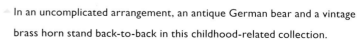

In an uncomplicated arrangement, an antique German bear and a vintage brass horn stand back-to-back in this childhood-related collection.

This collection of odds and ends is controlled by varying scale. Old typewriters on tabletops and brightly colored folk art fish tightly placed together on the wall, along with a very large contemporary tall-shade lamp, speak to one another due to their unique placements and scales.

Collections consist of items that somebody has a fondness for. A friend has numerous collections of tiny items arranged throughout her home. One that caught my eye was her collection of old Monopoly game pieces. Maybe it was their pewterlike finish, or interesting shapes, or even my childhood memories of the game that started me collecting the figurines too!

A collection of timepieces is organized and displayed in a harmonizing way. Antique dome-top jars containing clocks that range from an old alarm clock to vintage pocket watches are combined with stacks of silver-toned sugar tins and white saucers that add height and texture to the whimsical display.

My fondness for ironstone of any kind still continues today. In our farmhouse, placed in an old stepback cupboard is my collection of Victorian ironstone pitchers. To achieve a more modern look I added white wooden balls spaced evenly in a row between each piece, giving the display a simple but contemporary flair.

Old, tarnished pewter spoons resting on a sun-drenched tabletop cast the shadows of their unique weathered forms.

An antique folk art tin horse and cart is centered on the farmhouse table. The unique piece, which was collected for its weathered painted surface and one-of-a-kind handmade appeal, carries a polished red bocce ball, adding an unexpected design twist.

Colorful paperweights grouped tightly together form a collection based on organization and likeness. The clear, thick acrylic domes add a sculptural effect, while the abstract shapes of the different varieties of flowers create an artful visual.

Weathered granite garden ornaments add a modern flair to this outside space. The mottled gray spheres with their chunkiness and implied status add light and a repeating visual to the garden path.

Antique stores are great sources for garden decorations, with many specializing in items solely for the garden. Here, a collection of items with an airy, contemporary sensibility includes iron urns, various planters, and birdbaths that wait for their next abodes inside the house or out in the garden.

A long, tunnel-shaped tin florist vase with its richly painted green surface adds height and color to the outside patio table. The combination of these vintage collectibles works well because of the dull distressed patinas, unusual shapes, and varying statures.

A collection of antique porcelain items lines the mantel, giving an abstract, modern image to otherwise mundane kitchen pieces. The multiple patterns, shapes, and colors complement one another while the length of the display adds order.

An incredible blue- and green-painted primitive cupboard grounds a collection of antique folk art. A rooster weather vane placed off-center on the wall being paired with an oversize oil painting gives the space a gallery-like appearance while letting each piece be appreciated individually for its unique shape and patina.

A collection of white art pottery with crackled satin patinas is displayed simply in a row on a weathered tabletop, creating a unique contrast.

A collection of early porcelain in varying hues of whites and ivories fills the corner of the farmhouse. The all-white theme creates a soothing visual even though there are numerous differently shaped pieces with varying heights in the collection.

▶ Vintage porcelain light fixtures that once graced a bathroom wall are repurposed as modern art. When topped with marble spheres, the newly combined pieces create artistic sculptures that are appreciated for their bright white color, unique shape, and shiny texture.

Metal pieces, including furniture, factory hardware, and small decorative pieces, are highly sought after for their dull, pitted finishes, repurposed values, and industrial appeal. Here, a collection of vintage iron bicycle seats is placed on a zinc tabletop, creating an artistic vignette of shape and texture.

Unique collections based on color and form are eye-catching and interesting when added to a room's design. Here, a set of rubber-padded table-tennis paddles and an old iron industrial vent repurposed into a funky lamp work together because of their similar color and unique curved shapes. The old wall clock centers the collection by adding height and visual focus to the space.

Aqua-blue glass seltzer bottles are grouped on a weathered farm chair, creating a cheerful pop of color in the garden area.

In our Vermont kitchen I keep a collection of culinary brushes that are used for basting. I adore the soft colors of the natural bristles and the sculpted wooden handles. Here, an old, mottled colored ironstone bowl holds a large French pastry brush. The round shapes of both harmonize together while the brilliant blue-and-white towel with its bold stripes adds visual balance.

PARIS, 1867.

Mixed collections harmonize well together when their placement is correct. A vintage pair of iron bulls previously used as weights for windmills in the Midwest now are used as bookends, while a small tin pig and a copper sheep, both once weather vanes, are grouped with the bold, rectangular shapes of books and art that frame the repurposed collection of metal folk art.

Tarnished

Perfection

Chipped paint and tarnished silver tell stories. When arranged with pieces with contrasting textures, these unique characteristics may redefine your idea of perfection.

Glossy green paint covers the farmhouse's secondary staircase in the kitchen, giving a sleek appearance to the worn treads and risers. The wooden beadboard wall adds vertical lines while complementary yellows on the walls and trim add visual impact to the updated area.

Our golden retriever, Rooster, was conscientious even as a puppy. He took good care of his favorite toys and only once gave in to temptation and tested his puppy teeth on a chair leg. Years later, as he grew that characteristic old-dog white mask, those teeth marks became sentimental reminders of days long past. Rooster knew that his favorite bed was well worth the climb up the stairs. He was a cautiously confident stair climber, always choosing a path close to the wall. His morning descent always followed the same path. Over the years we started to notice that there was slight wearing in the painted stairs that marked Rooster's travel lane, always safely tight to the wall. Long after he made his last trip up the stairs with us, the scuffed treads remained. To paint them over would have erased something important: Rooster's presence in the house was one of the things that made it a home. Where the uninformed visitor may have seen the need for some touch-up paint, we saw only a gentle reminder of an old friend.

Chipped paint, cracks, and tarnish are the laugh lines and crow's-feet of furniture and furnishings. Unique character and nostalgia shine through tarnish; cracks and chips attest to the human touch, the passing of an object from hand to hand, and the passing of time.

Imagine the bright silver vase that began its journey as a treasured wedding gift, relegated years later to the back of the cupboard and eventually rediscovered by a favorite granddaughter, only to be inadvertently dented by the energetic great-grandson, then once again retired, this time to a box in the basement, and later liberated from the darkness and sold at a yard sale. These pieces will speak to you, and their stories are infinitely richer and more interesting than that of the bright new silver vase on the shelf.

I like to use worn pieces in my decorating; chipped paint played off against smooth chrome highlights the elements of both pieces. A piece of tarnished pewter juxtaposed with a brightly colored abstract painting may just catch your eye for long enough that you look again more closely. Mix textures, colors, and design styles to create a look that is unique to you and your home. And whatever you do, think twice before you reach for the touch-up paint or silver polish.

Our Vermont house's master bedroom is forty-five feet in length, which creates long vistas from both ends. Tucked under the knee wall at one end is a cottage bureau painted glossy white, with my favorite reads stacked on top. The vertical pine ceiling, also painted shiny white, sets the backdrop for a tarnished full-bodied copper eagle weather vane, creating a sculptural visual when looking down the lengthy room.

Unearthed apothecary bottles rich with dull patinas and mercury-tone colors reflect on a gleaming vintage spoon carved mirror, doubling the textures, flowing shapes, and soft colors.

This highly sought-after cow weather vane was rescued from the rooftop of the home owner's nearby barn. The gold-gilded bovine, with its sculpted metal form, is artistically placed on a tabletop between two unadorned windows. The simple placement highlights the form and finish of this newly recognized piece of art. Try combining finishes such as tin, steel, or iron with rusty or gilded surfaces for added layers of texture in your interior space.

I use primitive antique pieces in my design scheme as often as possible. I adore their boxy shapes, narrow widths, and worn colored finishes. In our Vermont living room, an early Pennsylvania pie safe clad in white paint and its original punched tin panels stands chest-high and centered on a long wall. A favorite contemporary painting given to me by a close friend is placed at eye level on the cupboard, drawing one's eye even closer to the space. Shiny gray painted wood floors add a soft reflective light while providing a neutral base for the designed area.

A large cement garden sphere covered in green moss and a weathered gray patina creates balance and adds an interesting shape to the living room arrangement.

A French garden urn revealing its many layers of paint was discovered and bought at a coastal antique store. The never-planted-in, heavy scrolled iron piece with a fluted base dominates a painted round table in the corner of my studio and is appreciated daily for its artistic value.

An early one-drawer blue table in its original finish creates a base for a white distressed boat hull in the farmhouse dining room. The worn textures of both are visually softened with the large red, white, and blue fabrics of the flag hanging above. Fabric added to a room setting, whether with upholstered furniture, drapes, or area rugs, will soften any "hard" space.

In my Vermont studio, a nineteenth-century cupboard used for art storage was once appreciated for its dark-red original finish. I gave it a more modern appearance by dry brushing multiple coats of white flat-finish paint over the dark old surface. When using this painting technique, make sure to apply the paint thinly so the dark imperfections in the wood are still visible to highlight the piece's worn, aged surface.

A silver-lustered collection of water pitchers and bowls
lines a hutch in the farmhouse, creating a reflective shine
of colors and mirrored shapes.

A vintage white porcelain sink is centered below a rustic six-pane window in the farmhouse kitchen. Placed in the sink area of the kitchen's work space are two topiaries of different heights arranged off-center to make a whimsical visual. The modern curved gooseneck faucet gleams in the afternoon sunlight, adding another texture to the space.

Simple but appealing, this weathered French bistro chair in the spring garden becomes a makeshift plant stand for a clay pot filled with thick-leaved succulents.

A transparent glass bowl cradles a group of paperwhite bulbs that are being forced to bloom early. The bowl adds a shiny texture to the arrangement while its transparency lets the brightly colored linen towel shine through for added graphic appeal. Sunlight absorbed by the bowl creates warmth, which is an added bonus that helps the plants to grow in the off-season.

Curved wooden chairs covered with lichens add a soft modern edge to the visual grid pattern created by the horizontal clapboards, the two-over-two window sash, and the intricate lines of the brick patio. The off-center placement of the table and chairs under the window is visually balanced by the myrtle topiary-filled planter, creating a casual abstract feel in the outdoor space.

A vintage patio dining room set found a new home inside an enclosed sunroom. The white-painted iron-frame chairs are softened by canvas-covered cushions with contrasting welting, while a gleaming glass tabletop adds an airy feeling to the area, all creating an illusion of space.

A collection of worn flowerpots, some with intricate cutout designs, are stacked and clustered together in the garden. The collection adds visual details to the space, with its mossy textures and cylindrical shapes.

This long, uninterrupted wall of our Vermont house creates the
perfect space for our vintage French dining set. The stone patio adds
an organic, rustic texture to the space, while the contemporary
smooth brick wall on the house's exterior creates a canvas for the
bold black manufactured lines of the table and chairs.

A rusted iron spring chair from the garden is appreciated for its sturdy construction, graphic lines, and bold shape. For year-round use inside, spray a coat of clear varnish on rusted areas and add a plump down-filled seat cushion in your favorite fabric.

A deep-welled ornate urn is topped with a boxwood wreath that was salvaged from a Christmas past, adding worn colors and soft textures to the hard surface of the cement garden vessel.

A ceramic-tile floor with its tight grid pattern contrasts valiantly with a finely carved side chair made of dark walnut. The bright blue round pillow adds color and a modern shape to the space.

A Victorian-era sofa with its heavily carved ornate arms is softened with a plain, modern blue fabric.

A tall chest with oversize drawers becomes the focal point in the farmhouse master bedroom. Admired for its original white distressed finish and contemporary boxy shape, the piece adds needed storage to the space while holding favorite collectibles on top.

My collection of rocking horses grows yearly. I found this carved horse
at an antique shop during my travels and knew instantly that it had
to come home with me. Because it was not in perfect condition and
lacked its original paint, I decided to give it an artistic makeover with
simple applications of paint in crisp, straight lines of blue, gray, and
white. It is now my favorite horse in the collection and is valued for
its unique abstract appearance.

I collect kitchen cutting boards for their unique formed handles, weathered surfaces, and different wood varieties. In our kitchen, you can find stacks of them at each end of our long work space, where they add warm wood tones along with a variety of eye-pleasing shapes and sizes.

Rule of thumb: Decorate kitchens only with kitchen-related items. Here, antique French pudding molds add repetitive designs and a metal texture to this kitchen space. For a design statement in your kitchen, try multiples of your favorite collectibles lined up in a row or stacked high for an even greater effect.

Antique French silver domed serving pieces paired with mismatched cutlery grouped on a platter are placed in the dining space to create a casual atmosphere, while a graphic linen cloth adds an abstract quality to the table vignette.

A pastry tin made of multiple rectangles makes an appealing cradle for eggs in the kitchen.

Space creates a modern approach in any room. In a friend's den, the walls are lined with dental trim and other ornate moldings. A textural rattan side chair placed between two windows is just enough for this otherwise visually powerful background, while a brightly colored architectural landscape painting adds dimension, as if creating a third window. Hanging art low on walls gives the room a gallery feel and exhibits the art to the fullest extent possible.

An upstairs-hall sleeping nook lined with rustic hewn beams is softened by the linen damask fabric while naive art is tucked in on an end wall as a makeshift headboard.

A farmhouse guest bedroom has been transformed with modern furnishings. Shiny ceramic surfaces in bright colors harmonize with soft linen fabrics and formal antiques, creating an abstract vignette that works based on its organization of repeating shapes and colors.

An upholstered headboard bearing a contemporary circle
pattern harmonizes with the deep yellow bed pillows.
The rustic metal bedside table with its wooden scrubbed
top complements the glossy mid-century bedside lamp while
also repeating the circular shape in the headboard fabric.

A small oil painting is placed far to one side of the mantle, coaxing your eye toward the wood details of the door and trim, while the blue hues from the art pull similar colors from the layers of chipped paint on the mantle to create a harmonizing vignette.

A collection of white corals and porcelain is highlighted by the dark shadows created by the late-afternoon sun. Being aware of reflective light in a room is very important when planning a design scheme: southern light produces harsher shadows, while northern light casts a softer filtered light.

Mixing design styles creates impact in a room. Here, a chipped decorated crock, now used as a decorative planter, is combined with modern canvas chairs that surround a glossy painted table. Fresh pears add an organic shape, texture, and color to the airy dining space.

A blue willow sugar bowl long missing its cover now holds white taper candles in the farmhouse kitchen.

Nubby rough-linen pillows add color and comfort to this seating area. The custom-designed button enclosures on the pillows are delightful and create another layer of texture.

In our Vermont house, a pair of linen-covered wing chairs have an updated look when combined with one of my large abstract paintings. A rustic chest made from weathered crates contrasts with the modern silver desk lamp, creating a play on textures and styles.

This bar crowned with collectibles has many different textures. The mid-century clock vase's reflective silver finish, the dull-metal aluminum ice bucket, and the shiny glass seltzer bottle are finishes that harmonize well together.

SPECIAL
50¢

These large-scale lamps made of old iron balusters from a row-house railing add sculptural design and height to this tabletop grouping of seacoast-related collectibles.

The original old, dry surfaces of this upstairs farmhouse hallway are appreciated for their artistic value. The weathered tones of the wood door and trim, paired with the patina on the well-worn floor along with the mottled white plaster walls, decorate with texture alone.

Exposed rustic beams create a graphic design in this farmhouse kitchen. A neutral-finish dining table with chairs adds a modern industrial feel to the room, while the tone-on-tone doors combined with the simple art create subtle patterns in the background.

Scale sometimes can be more important than the actual design pieces in a room. Here, oversize paintings arranged side by side command the space over the fireplace mantle, while the two Tiffany clocks, small in scale, actually draw your eye into the space, making them the focal point rather than the large art.

The complex lines of an industrial laundry basket paired with the brushstrokes of the abstract painting hanging above it complement one another in an artistic, modern way.

I am constantly on the hunt for weathered antique wooden finials. I'm fond of their layers of chipped paint, dramatic carved shapes, and the powerful sense of design they can add to a room. This collection, placed high atop a cupboard, is grouped and appreciated as fine abstract art.

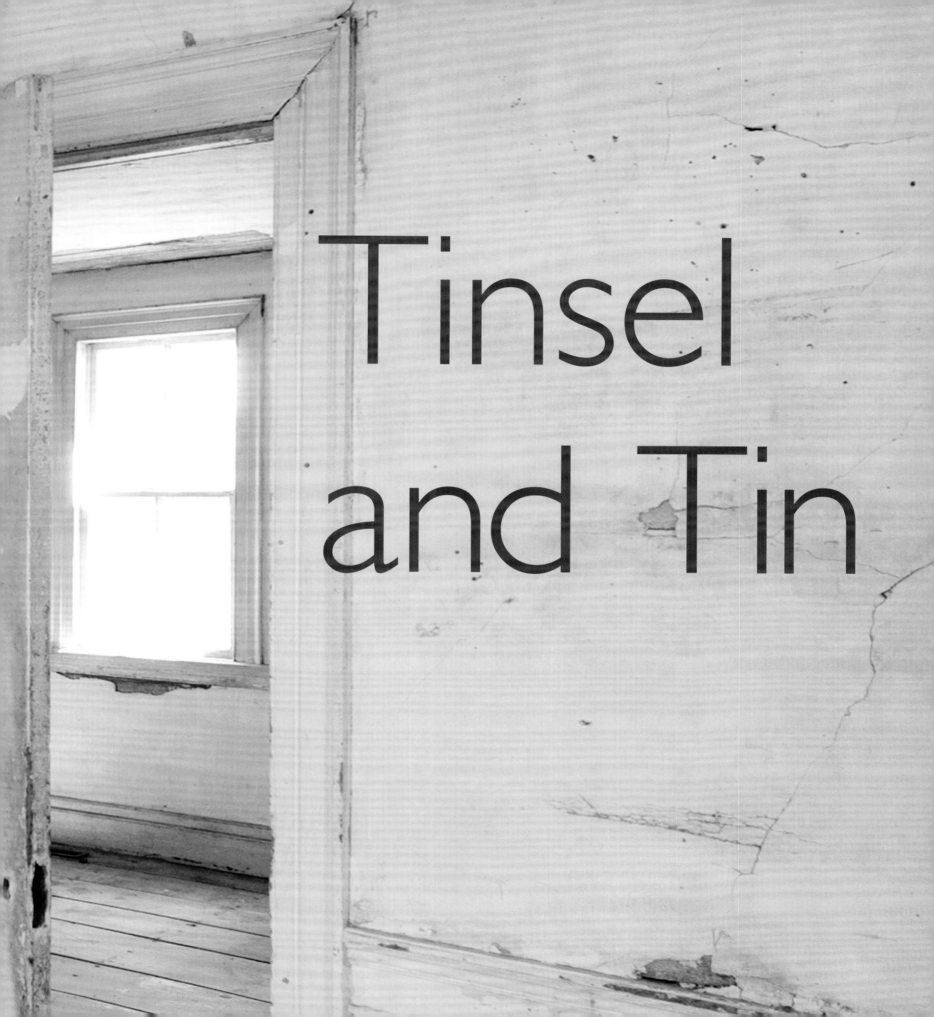

Tinsel and Tin

Showcase your traditional holiday decorations by creating artistic, playful combinations. Infusing an element of surprise into your seasonal designs can renew tradition.

A pale blue cupboard with multiple plank doors is centered along a large wall in our Vermont house's dining room. It is appreciated for its large scale, pop of energetic color, and the grounding effect it creates for the primitive white rocking horse dressed with a simple holiday wreath. The round, modern spheres add an unexpected abstract element to the weathered farmhouse pieces.

To me, celebrating Christmas is a personal experience. There are the larger celebrations that light up villages and cities around the world; then there are the quiet times in our homes where we acknowledge our own traditions and celebrate the season surrounded by friends and family.

Some find comfort in tradition and enjoy unpacking the holiday boxes and carefully re-creating years of holiday decorating. Everything has its place because that is the way it has always been! For those with a good memory, holiday decorating can be accomplished in a few hours. This here, that there, and done.

I enjoy the opportunity that comes with the holidays to decorate and create temporary seasonal designs that at any other time of year would fall into the category of "over the top." A season that embraces the idea of dragging a tree into your home and covering it with lights and glitter simply can't last long enough for me! Think of the quiet, conforming neighbor who, once possessed by the spirit of the season, transforms a modest unassuming home into the theatrical display of color and holiday cheer. Anything is fair game for adorning with a string of lights, swag of greens, gift wrap, or bow; nothing is off-limits! Our pets tolerate the holiday collars, and we feel inspired to wear silly hats and sweaters that are acceptable only when under the influence of the holiday spirit.

As with the rest of my design, I like to mix things up and work the vintage and traditional in alongside the modern and edgy to create unexpected vignettes and design details that catch the eye. Once green and fragrant, the skeletal remains of last year's Christmas tree can reappear this year with a fresh covering of silver spray paint. By refocusing on form rather than on the traditional attributes by which we judge Christmas trees, this natural sculpture can take on a new life and, in truth, may be more interesting this time around than when it stood in the corner draped in tinsel.

This year, consider saving some of your cherished ornaments to use as accent pieces around your home. Twine spools painted silver can serve as nontraditional platforms for these traditional pieces. Place the ornaments on the spools and arrange them on your mantel or showcase them elsewhere in your home for a colorful holiday display. You will appreciate these ornaments all over again when you see them in an unexpected setting.

Last Christmas, I discovered a bunch of those old flashbulbs that, though used, still maintain an interesting glassy-ice look. I mixed them in a bowl with a handful of small white boiling onions to see what sort of reaction they would solicit. The contrasting textures of the natural onion skins and the smooth, glassy bulbs created a whimsical effect worthy of a second look. Holiday guests are quickly learning to look closely and expect the unexpected in my seasonal decorations.

Consider your own collections and see if they might be worked into your holiday decorating. Dust off the piece that is waiting for just the right space and create a personal, one-of-a-kind design that tells more about you than where you shop for holiday decorations.

White carved wooden doves mixed with hearty evergreen boughs adds a natural look to the holiday centerpiece. The large distressed finial complements its surroundings, creating a sense of harmony with the other white furnishings while adding a soft round shape to the space.

I have collected sterling silver candlesticks for many years. I like their simple approach and visual impact, especially when grouped together on a tabletop as a center visual. For several holiday seasons now, I've intertwined French paper ribbon with Christmas-spirited words boldly printed on it. Make sure to use white unscented taper candles, as they do not compete with but rather complement the glimmering silver finishes of the candlesticks of various heights.

A round oak pedestal table serves as a wreath-making station in the barn attached to the farmhouse. I favor freshly picked balsam wreathes with no ribbon or decorations for their simplicity, incredible scent, and natural feathery form.

Small evergreen trees planted in galvanized tin pots are casually arranged on the brick walk leading to the side entrance of the farmhouse.

This cement dog has been with us forever, moved time and again, and always placed by the front entrance of our home. During the winter season he stands guard wearing a boxwood wreath as a whimsical collar, welcoming all who arrive for a visit.

Repurposed cardboard spools take on a new form as contemporary Christmas trees. The spools were sprayed with multiple coats of silver metallic paint and topped with antique glass ornaments to create this futuristic metal-finish holiday theme.

Long-needled Scotch pine boughs are intertwined among a collection
of English ironstone water pitchers, adding texture, contrast, and scent
throughout the holiday season.

A freshly cut naturally grown balsam tree with its uneven foliage and
sweet holiday scent fills our Vermont house's dining room. Decorated
simply with tiny white lights, the tree softly illuminates the room during
the festive holiday dinner parties that are held throughout the Christmas
season.

A huge wreath overwhelms the space over the den's mantel. The large-scale
greenery mixed with the petite French chair, clean-lined window, and modern
lamp creates a play on scale and adds balance to the small room.

A white column is topped with an old wooden finial that once graced the gazebo at our Maine summerhouse. Combining the two is a perfect marriage of their common distressed finishes and powerfully visual shapes. The small handmade boxwood wreath hung with a simple ribbon adds color to the whimsical holiday scene.

A broken string of early glass baubles that once graced a holiday tree now hangs as shimmering art glass on an old primitive wall cupboard.

An early blue-decorated cream pitcher holds a group of vintage Victorian glass holiday picks. The explosion of colors from the tiny spheres adds interest to the farmhouse cupboard.

Old tin candleholders that once graced our Christmas tree are added to a table centerpiece made of spruce boughs, ocean rocks, and colorful handblown glass ornaments. Make sure to always keep candles under your watchful eye.

Creative placement of wreaths will add interest and fresh woodland aromas to your home during the holiday season. Here, an old Windsor chair in chipped white paint cradles a freshly made cedar wreath with minimal decorations. Wreaths also make great centerpieces when laid flat on tabletops and filled with fruits, holiday cookies, or candles.

A silk tablecloth with bold patterns of blue and white sets the backdrop for a colorful group of small antique glass ornaments.

Our kitchen is always decorated with creativity during the holiday season. Here, a collection of simple ironstone bowls holds sweet white onions combined with repurposed blue and white mid-century flashbulbs that resemble fine handblown glass ornaments. Whimsy at its best!

An early German Santa sits on his original glittered ornament. Simply placed on a cloud of cotton batting, he adds cheer to the farmhouse during the holiday season.

Woodland decorations are a favorite of mine, and they fill our farmhouse during the holiday season. Here, a collection of early English ironstone pitchers is highlighted with natural pinecones that add contrasting color and form to this textural vignette.

Simple white cyclamens with a sweet scent are planted in vintage clay pots and are a favorite at the farmhouse during the Christmas season.

Fragrant cedar boughs casually twist along the railing in the front entry hall of the farmhouse. Fresh lemons intertwined with the greenery add yellow splashes of color, while an old weathered sled suggests pleasurable outings in seasons past.

An evergreen seedling of a simple form and pale green color creates a soft texture against the weathered wood walls in the background.

A collection of reproduction German Santas displayed and appreciated for their repetitive forms creates a contemporary installation on the mantle of the primitive farmhouse.

Rustic iron sheep wearing tiny brass bells are arranged in a straight line, lending simplicity to the collection.

Acknowledgments

Art Smith and Linda Zukas

Tony Elliott

Scott Smith

Lenny and Jenny Wellenius

Steve and Jody Hall

Mark and Leann Hodgson

Cindy Drane

Marvin and Ann Collier

Kenneth Blaisdell

Claire Hooper

Gwen Miller Dennis

Will Tanner and Thom Sacco

Bob and Caroline Boniello

Donald Poland and Jack Carew

Sandy Runnion

Tricia Rose

Tom and Julie Bonneville

Chris and Heather Woodell

John and Alecia Tolosky

John and GiGi Sjulander

Resources

Smith-Zukas Antiques
1755 Post Road
Wells, Maine 03902
www.smithzukasantiques.com

Snug Harbor Farm
Route 9
Kennebunk, Maine 04043
www.snugharborfarm.com

Camp Wool
42 Main Street
Kennebunk, ME 04043
207-985-0030
Toll Free: 1-866-938-WOOL
www.campwool.com

Lampscapes
77 Gates Street
White River Junction, Vermont 05001
www.lampscapes.com

Will Tanner Interiors
1 Lydon Lane
Cape Elizabeth, Maine 04107
www.willtannerinteriors.com

Columbary House Antiques
1286 US Route 1
Cape Neddick, Maine 03902
www.columbaryhouse.com

Tricia Rose
Rough Linen
415-577-8589
www.roughlinen.com

Bell Farm
244 US Route 1
York, Maine 03909
www.bellfarmantiques.com

Custom House Antiques
43 Main Street
Limerick, Maine 04048
207-793-8788

4 Main Street Antiques
4 Main Street
Cherryfield, Maine 04662
207-546-2664

Stone House Antique Center
557 Vt Route 103 South
Chester, Vermont 05143
802-875-4477

Withington and Company Antiques
611 US Route 1
York, Maine 03909
www.withingtonandcompanyantiques.com

Cornish Trading Company
19 Main Street
Cornish, Maine 04020
www.cornishtrading.com

Cooper, Angus, and Tyler wait patiently by the farmhouse door after a romp in the winter snow.